This
Read, Listen, & Wonder
book belongs to:

CANDLEWICK PRESS

To Cary and April
P. H.
To Kitty
K. L.

Text copyright © 1993 by Peter Hansard
Illustrations copyright © 1993 by Kenneth Lilly

First U.S. paperback edition with CD 2008

The Library of Congress has cataloged the hardcover edition as follows:
Hansard, Peter.
A field full of horses / Peter Hansard ; illustrated by Kenneth Lilly.—1st U.S. ed.
(Read and wonder)
Summary: Text and illustrations describe horse behavior, biology, and care.
ISBN 978-1-56402-302-5 (hardcover)
1. Horses—Juvenile literature. 2. Horses—Behavior—Juvenile literature. [1. Horses.]
I. Lilly, Kenneth, ill. II. Title. III. Series.
SF302.H35 1994 92-45830
636. 1—dc20

ISBN 978-0-7636-1434-8 (paperback)
ISBN 978-0-7636-3828-3 (paperback with CD)

2 4 6 8 10 9 7 5 3 1

Printed in China

The illustrations were done in pencil and watercolor.

Candlewick Press
2067 Massachusetts Avenue
Cambridge, Massachusetts 02140

visit us at www.candlewick.com

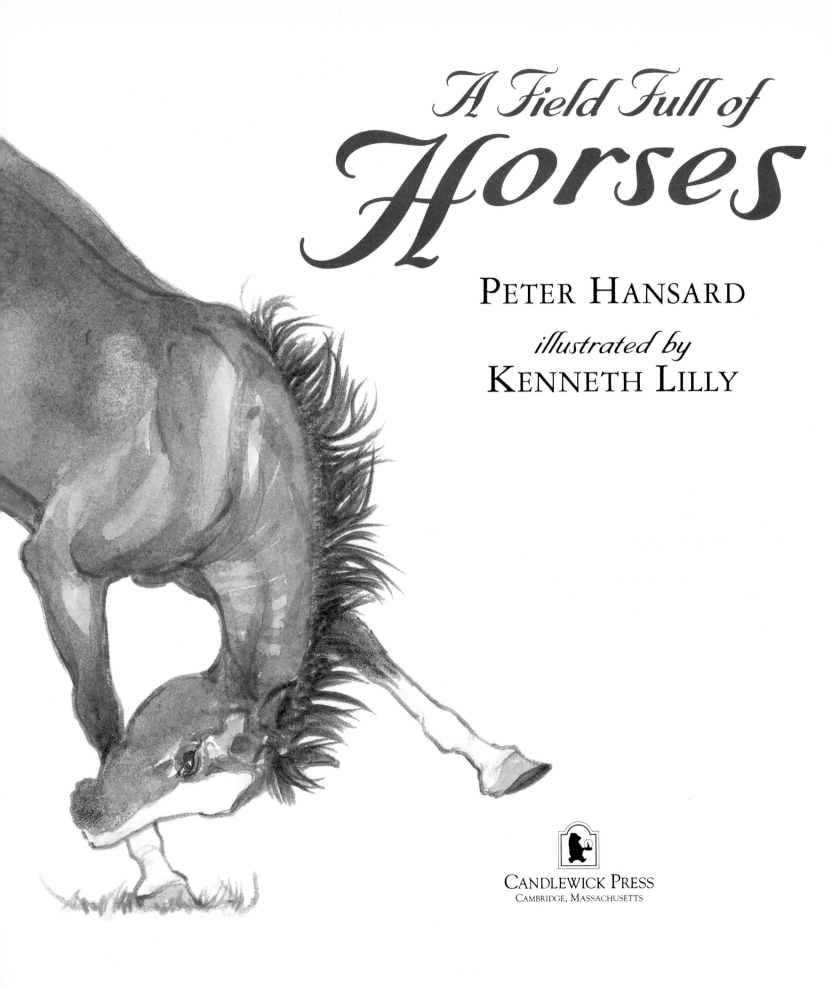

A Field Full of
Horses

PETER HANSARD

illustrated by
KENNETH LILLY

CANDLEWICK PRESS
CAMBRIDGE, MASSACHUSETTS

I walk along the winding lane,
past the tangled willows.
I climb up on the five-barred gate and . . .

there they are.
There's nothing I'd rather do
than just sit and look at horses.

One stands and stamps
in a timothy patch.

One crops the grass with
a champing sound.

In summer,
horses that live outside eat a lot of grass.
In winter, they're given rolled oats,
barley, bran, and hay.

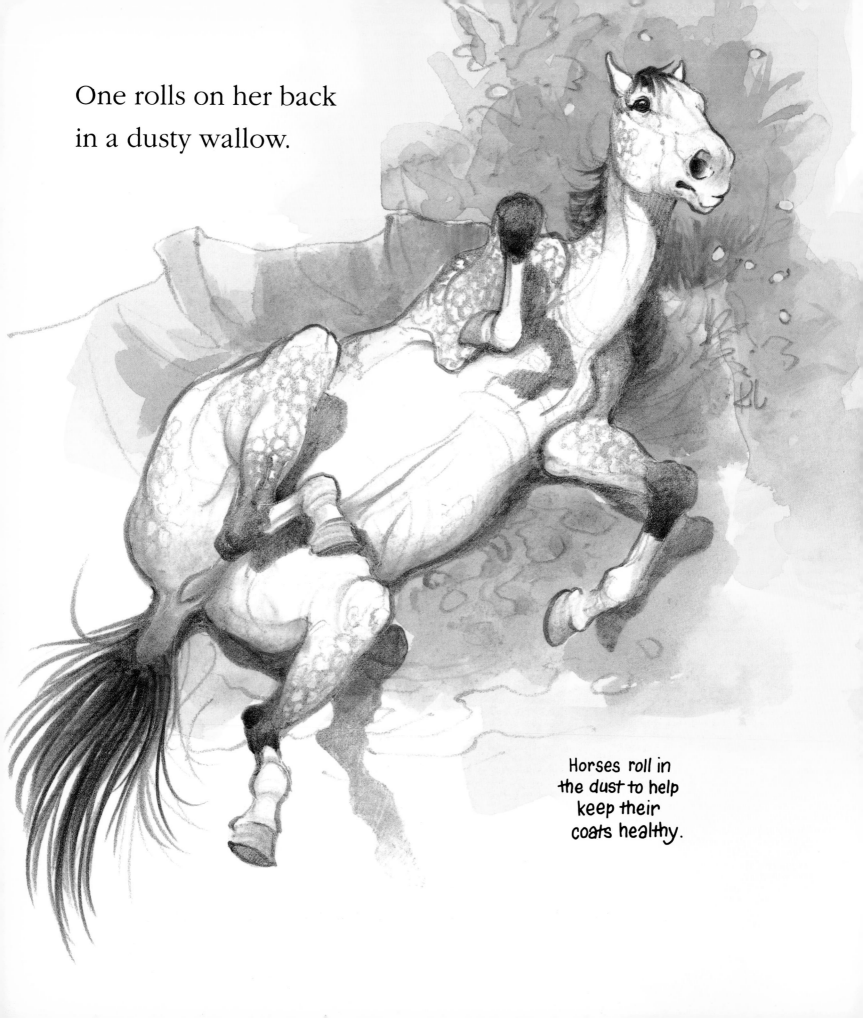

One rolls on her back
in a dusty wallow.

Horses roll in
the dust to help
keep their
coats healthy.

curry comb

dandy brush

hoof oil

HOOF OIL

hoof pick

sponge

body brush

Back at the stables, their owners groom them with tools like these.

One dreams in the shade of a big copper beech with eyes half shut and tail slowly swishing.

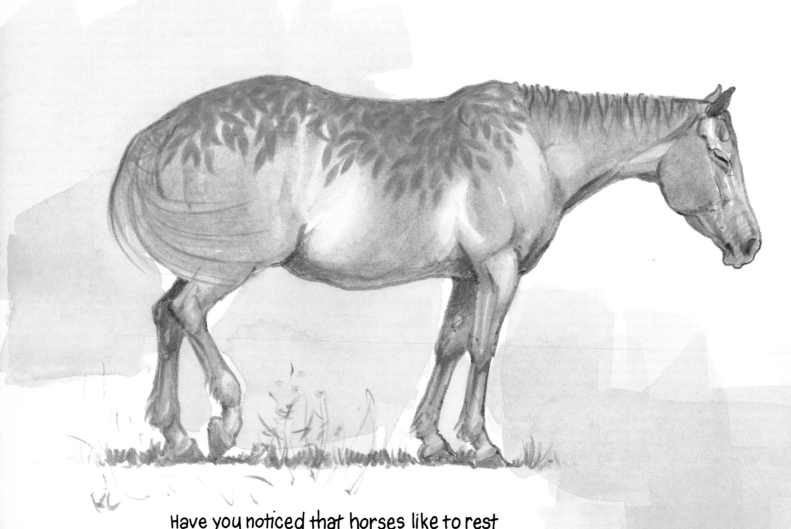

Have you noticed that horses like to rest with one hind foot up on a turned-back hoof?

One trots up to see if I have apples in my pockets.
She's my favorite and I wish that she were mine.

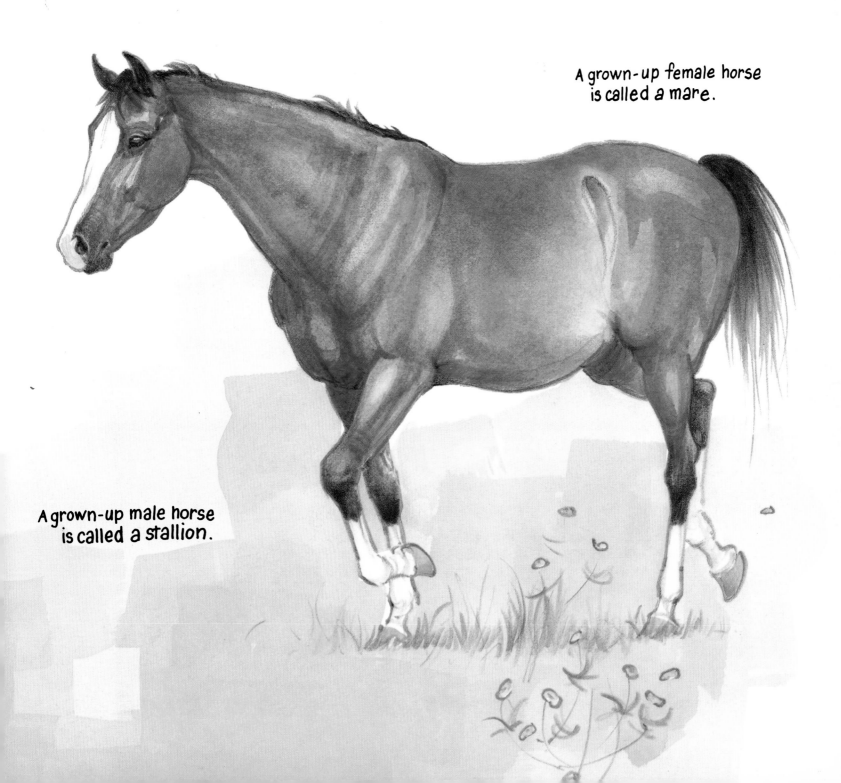

A grown-up female horse
is called a mare.

A grown-up male horse
is called a stallion.

Her eyes are big and soft, her nostrils flared
and sniffing, and every now and then
she gives a sudden shiver
to keep the flies away.

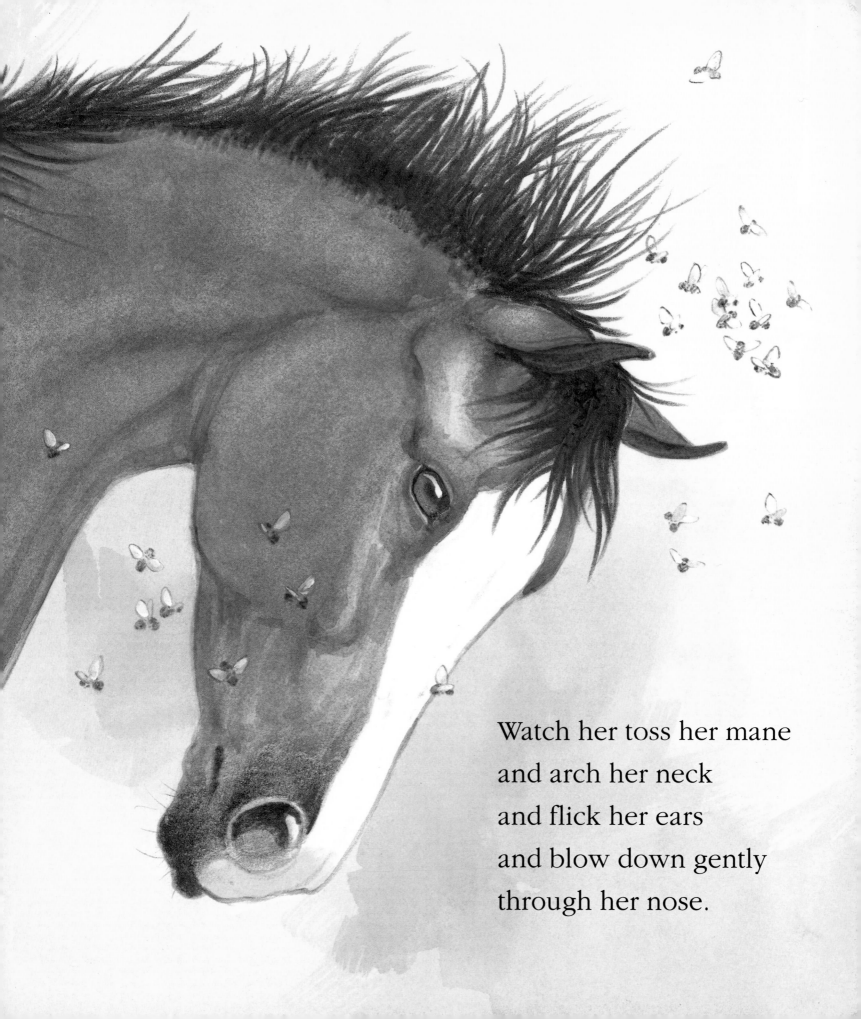

Watch her toss her mane
and arch her neck
and flick her ears
and blow down gently
through her nose.

Would you like to touch
her twitching nose?
It's silky soft,
but bristly too.

Would you like to make
the sounds she makes?
Horses whinny, horses snuffle,
horses nicker, snort, and neigh.

I love to smell her horsey smell.

It makes me think of muck and straw,

of earth and leaves and grass.

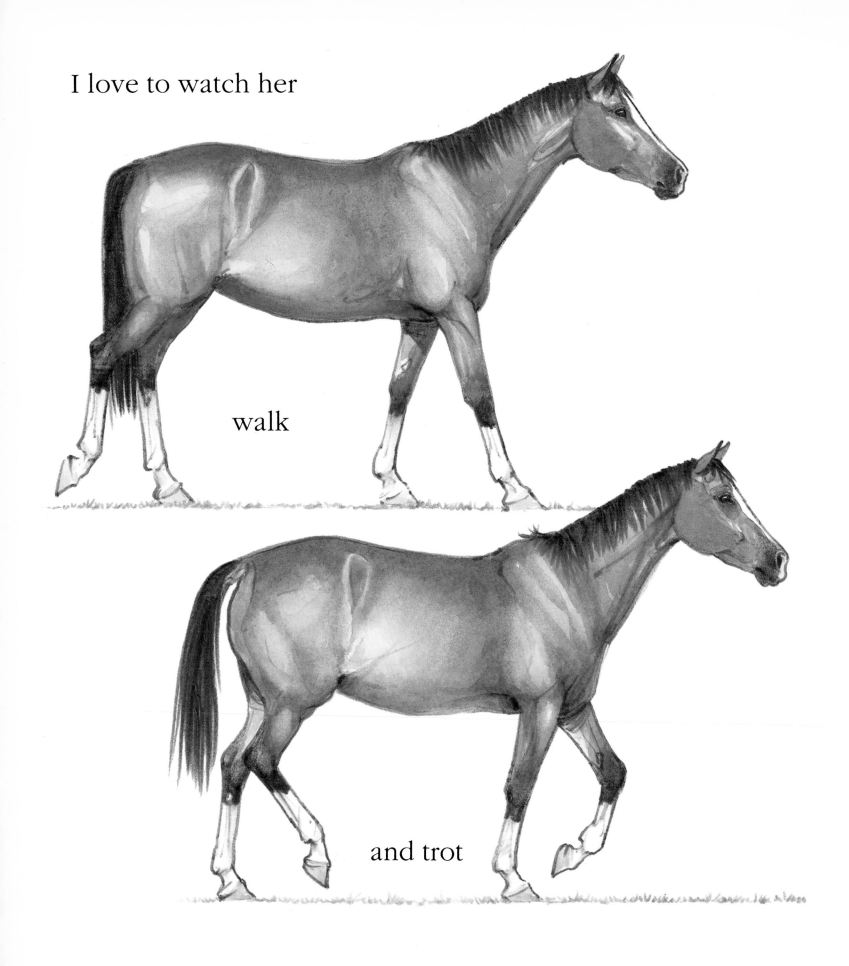

I love to watch her

walk

and trot

and canter

and gallop.

I love to watch her

buck

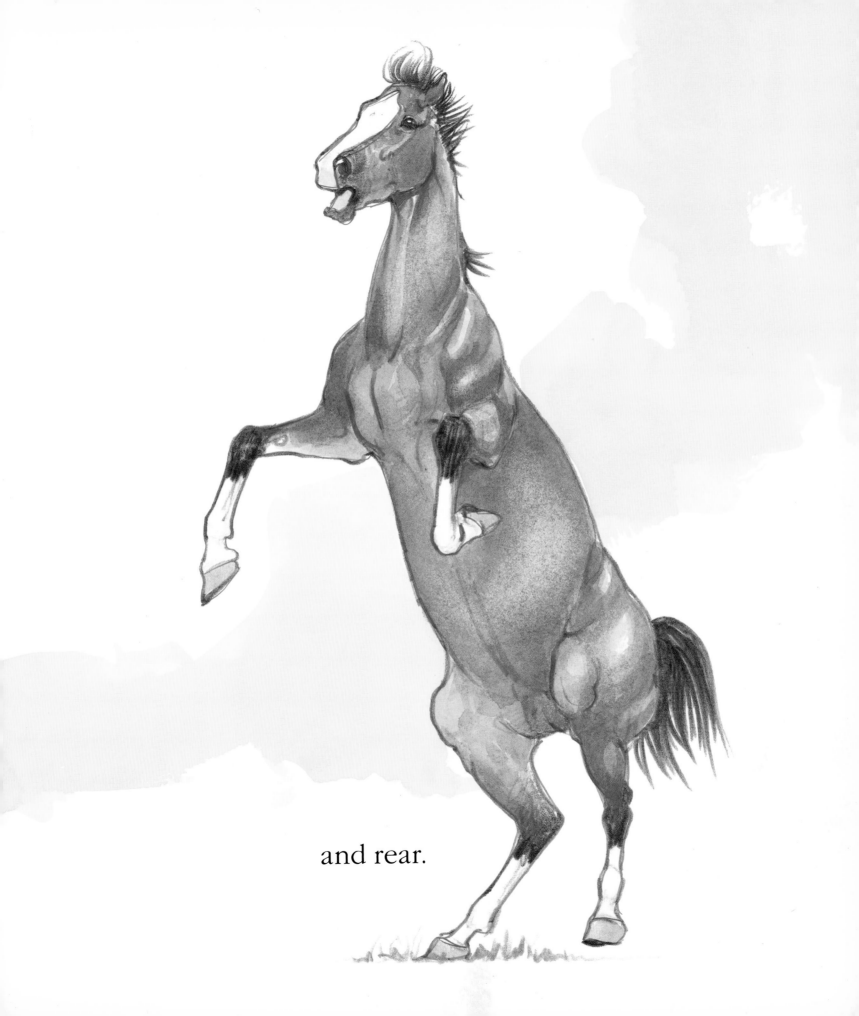

and rear.

I even love to watch her
standing still.

Poll

Mane

Withers

Forelock

Neck

Nostril

Muzzle

Shoulder

Breast

Chest

Chestnut

Knee

Cannon bone

Fetlock

Pastern

A horse is measured in HANDS, from the withers to the ground. One hand equals 4 inches.

A horse that measures less than 14 hands 2 inches from the withers to the ground is called a pony.

I love to watch her with her foal.

His head is small,

his body's short,

his legs are very long.

He jumps and kicks and starts to run.

And stops.

And dashes in a circle.

A newborn foal is wobbly on its feet
at first but quickly learns to walk.

If you could choose any horse,
which color would it be?

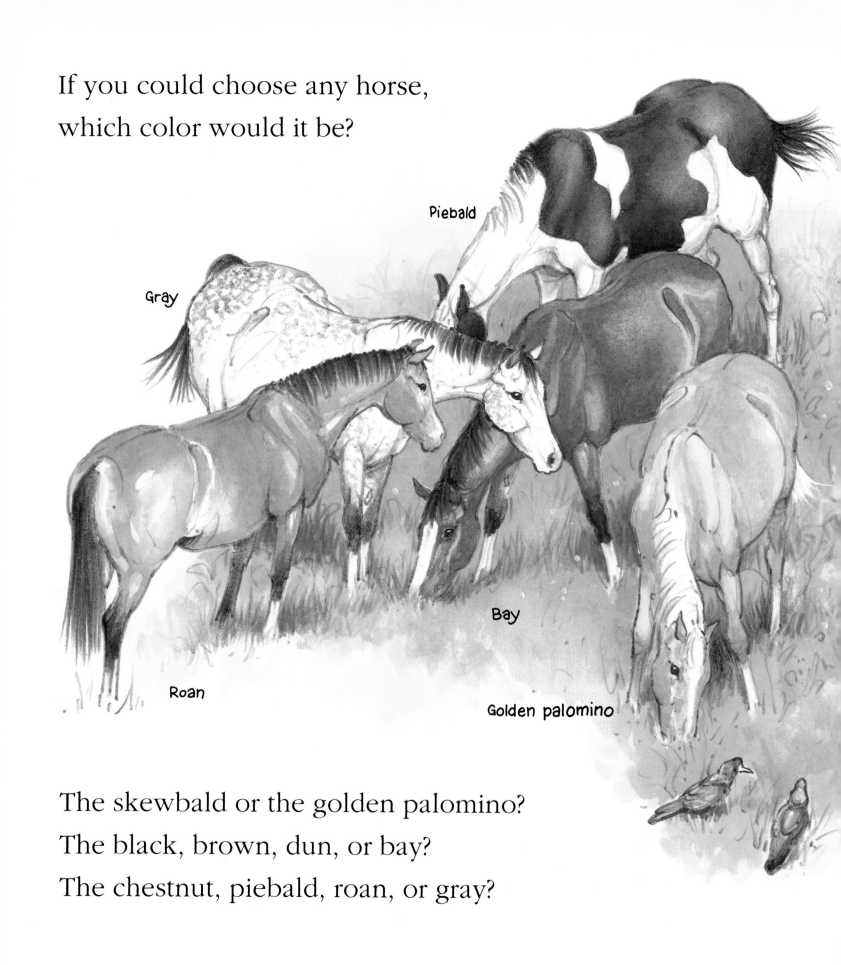

Piebald

Gray

Bay

Roan

Golden palomino

The skewbald or the golden palomino?
The black, brown, dun, or bay?
The chestnut, piebald, roan, or gray?

I have my favorite, but I love them all.
There's nothing I'd rather do
than just sit and be with horses.

Anglo-Arab

Dartmoor

Suffolk Punch

Holstein

Brabant

*There are many horses to look at inside this book—which one is **your** favorite?*

Breton

Tennessee Walker

Quarter Horse

Morgan

Arab

Hanoverian

Australian Stock Horse

Mustang

Salerno

Icelandic Horse

Connemara

Irish Draught

PETER HANSARD took children with him when he went to do research for this book. "We went to a nearby field," he explains, "and I watched to see what interested the children most. Then I created an 'ideal' paddock for the book, filled with all shapes and sizes of horses, so that I could show as much about them as possible."

Fjord Pony

Friesian

KENNETH LILLY'S grandfather was a farmer who trained horses, so he has been around them his entire life. In fact, it is family lore that as an infant he managed to crawl out of the garden and through a stable of twenty-one enormous farm horses. He was later found seated in the last stall, next to a horse happily eating its oats.

Camargue

Appaloosa

Percheron

Welsh Mountain Pony

Ardennais